THE EDUCATIONAL WORK

OF

The Birmingham and Midland Institute.

A PAPER

READ BEFORE THE SOCIAL SCIENCE ASSOCIATION,

AT ITS

MEETING IN BIRMINGHAM, IN OCTOBER, 1868.

(REVISED AND COMPLETED TO 31st DECEMBER, 1869,)

BY

Edwin Smith, Secretary.

PRINTED BY ORDER OF THE COUNCIL OF THE INSTITUTE FOR DISTRIBUTION TO THE SUBSCRIBERS

BIRMINGHAM:
PRINTED BY W. G. MOORE & Co., GAZETTE BUILDINGS, HIGH STREET.
1870.

THE EDUCATIONAL WORK

OF

THE BIRMINGHAM AND MIDLAND INSTITUTE.

THE BIRMINGHAM AND MIDLAND INSTITUTE was founded for educational purposes in 1853. A site for the building was granted by the Corporation of the Borough, and the sum of £17,500 has been obtained by public subscriptions and expended in the erection of the building, and in the purchase of the fittings and apparatus required to carry out the intentions of the founders.

The work of the Institute has always been carried on in two divisions, known as the General and Industrial Departments. In the General Department weekly lectures on scientific or literary subjects, a news-room, a yearly conversazione, and occasional courses of afternoon lectures, are provided. To these, subscribers of £1 1s. per annum are entitled to admission. The Industrial Department consists exclusively of classes for the study of Science, Arithmetic, Mathematics, Languages, English History, Literature, and Grammar and Composition, and Singing. The fee for admission to most of these classes is 3s. a term, or 9s. a year. There are, however, some classes to which the admission is one penny a lesson, and in one class—the Practical Chemistry Class—the fee is 7s. 6d. a term. The classes meet from October to June, and are closed during the Summer months. All of them are open to Females.

As the object of this paper is to give some idea of the extent of the work of the Industrial Department, which is the strictly educational division, no reference will be made in it to the work of the General Department, beyond the following short statement of its progress.

In 1855 there were 195 annual subscribers of £1 1s. each, entitled to the privileges of the General Department, and the income of the Institute was £310.

In 1858 there were 595 subscribers of £1 1s., and 49 subscribers of less amounts, entitled to the same privileges, and the income was £845.

In 1868 there were 1,077 subscribers of £1 1s., and 274 subscribers of less amounts, and the income was £1,367.

It should be stated that these amounts do not include the fees paid by Students in the Industrial Department.

As the present building was not completed until 1858, all the classes formed before that year were held in rooms temporarily engaged for the purpose. Owing to the limited income which was at first at the disposal of the Council, and to the experimental character of the work in which they were engaged, the Industrial

Department was opened in 1855 with three classes only. In the following year, seven additional classes were formed. From the imperfect character of the earlier registers, no information as to the classes, except the number of entries, can now be obtained. The following table shews the attendance at each class in the first term of the Sessions of 1855 and 1856.

	1855.	1856.
Physics	21	29
Chemistry	44	58
Physiology	20	Discontinued.
Arithmetic	—	21
Algebra	—	4
Geometry	—	4
Latin	—	11
French	—	146
English History	—	33
English Literature	—	62
Language and Thought	—	43
Logic	—	10
Totals	85	421

In 1857 a register was opened for the purpose of recording the names, residences, ages, and occupations of the students. From this register the accompanying Table of their occupations has been compiled. It must be explained that the figures given refer in all cases to the Autumn Term of the year named, the course of instruction in each class, always beginning with that Term. All Students earning their living by manual labour are placed in the first column, which includes Tool Makers, Die Sinkers, Brassfounders, Steel Toy Makers, Tin Plate Workers, Button Makers, Saw Piercers, Screw Makers, Metal Spinners, Pattern Makers, Gas Fitters, Lamp Makers, Wire Workers, Pen Makers, Rollers, Fitters, Japanners, Engine Fitters, Machinists, Electro Platers, Jewellers, Chasers, Engravers, Watchmakers, Carpenters, Builders, Masons, Coach Builders, Moulders, Carvers and Gilders, Cabinet Makers, Sawyers, Rule Makers, Plumbers, Coopers, Painters, Saddlers, Harness Makers, Printers, Opticians, Warehousemen, and Railway Porters and Pointsmen.

The second column includes Assistants and Apprentices to Tailors, Grocers, Barbers, Drapers, Shoe Makers, Ironmongers, Hosiers, Butchers, Bakers, Confectioners, Booksellers, Chemists, and Photographers.

It should also be noticed that many Students are included in the fourth and fifth columns who strictly belong to the Artisan Class, but as no particulars on this point are given in the registers, no accurate statement of the number can be made. It is estimated that one-half of the females now on the register are wives or daughters of Artisans, and that two-thirds of the Boys at School who are attending the classes are sons of Artisans.

The first division of this Table relates only to the classes to which the admission fee is paid quarterly. The fee to each of these classes being 3s. a Term, except, as before stated, to the Practical Chemistry Class.

The second division includes the classes to which the admission fee is one penny a lesson, but as no register, except of attendance, is kept in them, it should be noted that the figures given are only based upon an estimate. This estimate was most carefully made a few years ago by the Teachers of the classes and the Secretary of the Institute, and is the result of several weeks observation. As the Students were divided into three grades only, it must be remembered that the first column probably includes Boys at School, who would otherwise have been placed in the fifth column. They are in all such cases Boys belonging to the Artisan Class. The third column includes all male Students who are above the rank of Artisans. Few, however, belong to a higher class of Society than that under which they are ranked.

Some of the details given in this Table appear to be deserving of attention.

It will be seen that there has been a considerable fluctuation in the attendance at some of the classes. This is particularly marked in the Chemistry classes. It may be accounted for by the fact that the course of instruction in that subject extends over two years. It has always been noticed, since their establishment, that a large number of Students cease to attend as the teaching advances to the more difficult parts of the subject. In Class B, there was in this year a marked decrease in columns 1 and 2. This, it is believed, is in accordance with the experience of most of the leading Mechanics Institutes in the Kingdom, and leads to the inference that many Artisans who join science classes find, after a short attendance, that their elementary education has been insufficient to allow them to follow up any scientific study with the same advantage as Students belonging to a higher class of society.

Since 1857, the Chemistry Classes have been added to the list of penny classes. It is, perhaps, too soon to speak of the result of the experiment; there is, however, but little doubt, that this inference will be confirmed by the wider experience which will thus be gained in the teaching of Artisans.

In the French Class (opened in 1856) there appears to have been a larger number of Artisan Students in 1857 than in any later year. In 1858 the number had fallen off to about one-third of that of the previous year. This is doubtless due to the withdrawal of many of those Students who, it is found, will join any new class on its formation, but who cease to attend when they find that the study upon which they have entered presents greater difficulties than they had anticipated. Since 1858 the number of Artisans attending the class appears to have been about the same in each year. The fluctuations in the attendance of Shopmen may be partly attributed to the constant changes of employers and residence to which a large number of them are liable. A considerable diminution in the number of females attending this class took place in 1867. In that year there were only 22 on the register, in the previous year there were 60. On examination of the register it appears that in 1867 a large number of females, belonging principally to the class above the Artisans, ceased to be Students after an attendance of two or three or more years, and their places were not filled by new comers. Although there has been a slight increase in the number in the past year (1869), it is still far short of the number attending seven years ago. This seems to show that this language is now more efficiently taught in middle-class schools for girls, and a consequent decrease in the demand from females who have left school for such teaching.

The Latin Class was established in 1866 at the request of a large number of applicants for instruction in the language, the majority of whom were employed as Clerks in Solicitors' Offices. It will be seen that with one exception (in column 4) there has been a large falling off in every division. There is but little doubt that the decrease is owing to the reasons given for the decrease in the numbers attending the French Class. The number of females attending has been the same in each year, and it is gratifying to know, on the authority of the Teacher of the class, that the female Students are among the most earnest and hardworking of the Students. It may not be out of place to mention here that this is not the only class in the Institute in which this is the case.

The exceptionally large number of Artisan Students attending the English Literature Class in 1857, contrasted with later years, was doubtless owing to the class being then under the teachership of Mr. George Dawson. The falling off in all the divisions during the last few years may be accounted for by the numerous changes which have been made in the teachership. There has been a large increase in the attendance during the past year, and it is believed that it will soon recover its position in the class list.

The most noticeable increase in the numbers attending the quarterly classes has been in the Practical Chemistry, Mathematical, English Grammar, and Writing Classes.

The Practical Chemistry Class has grown so rapidly that the Council has been compelled on several occasions during the last few years to provide additional accommodation in the Laboratory, and the entries are now obliged to be limited to the number of Students whose work the teacher can at one time direct. During the past year there have been more applicants for admission to the class than can be taught, and the Council has made arrangements for the formation of an additional class at the beginning of the Winter Term of 1870. The largest increase has been in columns 1, 6, and 7.

The increase in the number of Schoolmasters attending is due to the recent regulations of the Science and Art Department, which enable Students who pass in the higher grades at the May examinations to earn payments on results in any classes which they may afterwards establish. And it may be here remarked that this is by no means the least important part of the work in which the Institute is engaged. Nearly all the Schoolmasters who have been so educated in the Institute during the past two or three years are now, or will be immediately, engaged in teaching science classes in their Schools, or elsewhere, in this and the adjacent Towns.

At Christmas, 1868, there were, according to the last report of the Science and Art Department, 446 individual Students attending Science Schools conducted mainly by Teachers who have been educated in the Midland Institute. During the past year this number has been largely increased; new Science Schools have been established in all parts of the town, the Teachers for which are frequently obtained from the Students in the Institute Classes. It ought to be remembered that without the Midland Institute, or a similar institution, to act as a normal school for the training of teachers, this work, or at any rate a very large portion of it, would never have been possible.

The increase in column 7 is owing to a larger number of manufacturers and their sons, engaged in the trades of the town, having recently become Students. It is perhaps desirable to explain that in Birmingham there are a large number of manufacturers engaged in trade who have but small establishments, and who, while employing a few journeymen, are themselves workers at their trade, occupying the position which would correspond with that of foreman in the manufactories of many other towns. Many of them are men who would not be able to pay a high fee for instruction, and who, without such an Institution as the Midland Institute, would be unable to obtain any scientific education. All such manufacturers are included in column 7. It is believed that in the Autumn Term of 1869 all the Students attending this class who are manufacturers of a higher position in society than those just referred to, are contributors to the funds of the Institute in other ways than by the payment of class fees.

In the Mathematical Classes the increase is perhaps attributable to a knowledge of mathematics being required for the study of sciences, and to some extent, bears out the inference drawn from the falling off of the number of Students in Chemistry as the course of instruction advances. The total increase in the number of Students attending these classes is also remarkable. In 1857 there were 19 Students; there are now 40.

The increase of Students in the Grammar Class is due to the increase in the number of Artisans and Clerks now attending the class. The small proportion of Students of a higher rank also tends to shew that the largest demand for elementary education for adults comes from the ranks of the Artisans.

During the past year there has been a large increase in the number of Clerks attending the Writing Class. The register shews that many of them are boys of 15 or 16, who would be more correctly classed as office or warehouse boys.

It will be seen that the largest proportionate increase in the number of Students has been in the Penny Classes. In the Elementary Arithmetic Class, which in 1857 had 21 Students only, there are now 145; in the Advanced Arithmetic Class, which was a quarterly one until 1865, there was an average attendance up to that year of 27, it is now 66; and in the Elementary Singing Class, which at its commencement had an average attendance of 116, there are now 407 Students.

Assuming the correctness of the division, it will be seen that there is a larger proportion of Artisans in these classes than in any of the others, and it is believed that a careful enquiry would prove that since this estimate was made the proportion of Artisan Students in these classes has rather increased than diminished.

The fee to the Chemistry Classes has lately been reduced to one penny a lesson. The result has been a considerable increase in the attendance, and a much larger attendance of Artisans. From the present short experience of the extension of the penny system to these classes, it is unfair to draw any inference as to the success of the experiment. One fact may however be noted; at the last May examination by the Science and Art Department, more Artisan Students presented themselves from this class than in any former year. It has yet to be seen whether the result of the second year's teaching (the more difficult part of the course of instruction) will show an equally favourable result. The numbers, referring to these classes given in the table, are based on a slightly different estimate to that referring to the other penny classes. It is found that but very few females attend. The Students have therefore been divided into two classes only, Artisans and Clerks, the latter including all Students above the rank of Artisans.

The totals in this table, while shewing that the number of Students has risen from 578 to 1,417 in ten years, also shews that the proportion, in most of the divisions, is about the same to the total number, as in 1857. It is, however, encouraging to find that the proportion of Students who are known to be Artisans has increased from 39 per cent. in 1857 to 45 per cent. in 1869.

The accompanying table (No. 2) gives the per centage of Students in the various classes grouped according to the subjects which are taught in them.

The following table, giving the numbers of Students of various ages, refers to the Quarterly Classes only. No information on this point can be given with regard to the Penny Classes :—

	Students between the Ages of				*Totals.*			
	14 and 20	20 and 30	30 and 40	40 and upwds				
SCIENCE CLASSES :—								
Practical Chemistry	18	13	6	3				
Experimental Physics	12	9	0	1				
Botany	8	2	2	2	59	36	15	8
Practical Mechanics	12	7	0	0				
Animal Physiology	3	3	3	1				
Practical Plane and Solid Geometry	6	2	4	1				
MATHEMATICAL CLASSES :—								
Algebra	8	12	0	0	19	21	0	0
Geometry	11	9	0	0				
LANGUAGE CLASSES :—								
French	78	31	5	0				
German	24	12	5	3	128	62	12	4
Latin	26	19	2	1				
ENGLISH CLASSES :—								
English Literature	8	12	2	0				
English History	3	6	1	0	94	90	11	1
English Grammar	38	49	6	0				
Writing	45	23	2	1				
SINGING CLASS	..	..	..	..	49	85	10	6
Totals					349	294	48	19

The register also shews that the greatest proportion of the Students attending the quarterly classes live within a distance of two miles from the Institute. In 1869 36 per cent. of the Students lived within one mile, 45 per cent. within two miles, 13 per cent. within three miles, and 6 per cent. lived at distances varying from three to twelve miles.

The satisfactory character of the work which is being carried on in the Institute Classes cannot perhaps be more clearly shewn than by the following statement. In 1861, the earliest year in which all the examinations now in operation were held, 122 Certificates and Prizes were awarded to Students in the Institute Classes, 33 of them being certificates from the Society of Arts and Science and Art Department. In 1869 the number was 342, of which 112 are awards from those bodies.

The rapid growth of some of the classes during the past few years has been in one way a source of difficulty to the Council of the Institute. Some of the most important classes are now obliged to be held in rooms quite unfitted for the purpose. While the number of Students was small, comfortable rooms could be provided for them, but now the want of large class rooms is sorely felt. There is not the slightest doubt that many of the Students who join the Classes at the beginning of the session are driven away because the class rooms are crowded with a larger number of Students than they were designed to accommodate, and are consequently ill ventilated and uncomfortable. For several years past Students wishing to join the Elementary Arithmetic Class at the beginning of the session have been turned away from the doors for want of room.

With larger class rooms, it is fully believed that much greater progress might be made in the Industrial Department during the next twelve years than has been accomplished in the past.

UP

	BC (Prob			REMARKS
59	1857	1867	1869	
	4	18	..	Established in 1863. } (*See* 1d. Classes.)
	..	. 6	..	
	0	15	36	
	2	14	22	
	..	19	14	Established in 1858.
	..	...	10	" in 1868.
	..	...	14	" in 1869.
	..	..7	..	" in 1867. (*See* 1d. Classes.)
	..	..4	19	" in 1863.
	0	8	20	
	0	3	20	
5	8	75	134	
	..	..30	44	Established in 1862.
	..	..47	48	Established in 1866.
4	0 }	12	10	These subjects were taught in one class in the years 1860, 1861, 1862, and 1863.
4	0 }	5	22	
	..	297	93	Established in 1859.
2	..	..48	71	Established in 1861.
	0	....	..	Discontinued in 1858.
7	..	c..	150	Established in 1859. Discontinued in 1861. Recommenced in 1866, but discontinued after meeting for one term. Again recommenced in 1869.
	..	. 7	..	Established in 1865. Discontinued in 1868.
5	14	2895	727	
	..	....	100	} Quarterly Classes until 1868-9.
	..	....	45	
	..	....	48	Quarterly Class until 1867-8.
3	0	c 50	66	This class was a quarterly one until 1865. It was then established on the 1d. system. It is included in this Table for the purposes of the summary.
	..	..124	145	
	..	..314	407	Established in 1863.
	..	..225	..	Discontinued temporarily to provide room for classes.
7	14	281308	1538	
1	2	4 ..	..	

TABLE 1.—OCCUPATIONS OF STUDE

Group	CLASS.	ARTISANS. 1857	1860	1862	1864	1866	1867	1869	SHOPMEN AND PPRENTICES. 1857	1860	1862	1864	1866	1867	1869
Science Classes.	Chemistry (Class A)	10	16	7	8	10	14	*	11	[illegible]	18	4	3	8	..
	" (Class B)	..	..	..	15	20	9	..	..	.	..	9	18	7	..
	Practical Chemistry	2	0	3	4	2	2	9	0		1	1	2	2	3
	Experimental Physics	6	9	5	12	6	8	4	1		2	3	1	1	2
	Botany	..	3	0	1	0	3	1	..		2	3	6	4	6
	Animal Physiology	..	..	..	..	..	..	5	..	.	..	..	..	..	0
	Practical Plane and Solid Geometry	..	..	..	..	..	..	8	..	.	..	..	..	..	0
	Physical Geography	..	..	..	..	..	8	*	..	.	..	..	..	0	..
	Practical Mechanics	..	..	..	11	12	11	8	..	.	..	0	0	0	0
Mathmcl. Classes.	Algebra	4	5	3	6	13	15	7	0		0	0	0	1	2
	Geometry	5	4	2	9	3	8	5	0		1	0	0	1	0
Language Classes.	French	42	13	22	20	21	18	23	19		20	11	21	11	7
	German	..	..	3	2	4	3	2	..	.	5	1	0	0	0
	Latin	..	..	..	..	18	7	9	..	.	..	..	9	5	2
English Classes.	History	6	4	4	3	2	6	1	3	[illegible]	5	2	3	0	0
	Literature	14			4	4	1	3	1			3	1	0	3
	Grammar	..	19	13	20	33	33	28	..	[illegible]	4	3	4	6	5
	Writing	..	..	17	20	24	17	21	..	..	4	7	3	4	4
Classes discontinued.	Logic	4	..	..	..	..	..	..	1	..	..	..	..	..	..
	Advanced Singing	..	3	..	..	6	..	48	..	[illegible]	..	..	1	..	5
	Geology	..	..	..	..	4	2	..	..	..	..	..	3	1	..
		93	76	79	135	182	165	182	36	[illegible]	62	47	75	51	39
Penny Classes.	Chemistry (Class A)	..	..	..	..	..	..	67	..	..	..	..	..	..	..
	" (Class B)	..	..	..	..	..	..	30	..	..	..	..	..	..	..
	Physical Geography	..	..	..	.	..	..	30	..	..	..	..	..	..	..
	Advanced Arithmetic	6	16	8	12	36	30	41	1	1	2	2	..	..	..
	Elementary "	12	34	58	78	63	75	87	..	..	..	..	..	..	..
	" Singing	..	..	..	69	165	189	245	..	..	..	..	..	..	..
	Penny Lectures	114	93	78	60	114	135	..	..	..	..	..	..	..	..
	Totals	225	219	223	354	560	594	682	37	31	64	49	75	51	39
	Per Centage	39	35	31	41	41	46	45	6	5	9	6	6	4	3

Group	CLASS.	CLERKS 1857	1860	1862	1864	1866	1867	1869	FEMALES (Occupations not ascertained, probably one-half are Daughters of Artisans). 1857	1860	1862	1864	1866	1867	1869
Science Classes.	Chemistry (Class A)	10	11	3	2	0	9	..	1	0	2	0	0	0	.
	" (Class B)	..	..	.	8	13	8	..	..	..	..	3	6	4	..
	Practical Chemistry	1	1	2	0	3	4	5	1	0	0	0	1	1	2
	Experimental Physics	6	7	1	3	3	6	7	0	0	0	1	0	0	1
	Botany	..	0	1	2	3	1	2	..	3	1	0	2	1	0
	Animal Physiology	..	..	..	..	..	..	2	..	..	..	..	..	..	0
	Practical Plane and Solid Geometry	..	..	..	..	..	..	4	..	..	..	..	..	..	0
	Physical Geography	..	..	..	..	..	2	..	..	..	..	..	..	2	..
	Practical Mechanics	..	..	..	3	3	4	4	..	..	..	0	0	0	0
Mathmcl. Classes.	Algebra	2	6	4	1	6	9	7	0	0	0	0	1	0	0
	Geometry	5	2	3	2	4	2	9	0	0	0	0	2	0	0
Language Classes.	French	46	59	70	60	58	53	54	46	44	60	53	60	22	35
	German	..	..	17	10	15	13	25	..	..	17	14	8	9	9
	Latin	..	..	..	..	42	19	19	..	..	..	..	11	11	11
English Classes.	History	9	4	8	8	5	5	5	0	1	4	4	0	1	4
	Literature	14			9	10	4	11	6			3	2	0	4
	Grammar	..	21	14	11	35	43	37	..	16	5	15	25	12	21
	Writing	..	..	10	1	7	4	13	..	..	18	10	18	20	32
Classes discontinued.	Logic	8	..	..	..	..	..	..	0	..	..	..	..	..	..
	Advanced Singing	..	5	..	..	4	..	25	..	7	..	..	8	..	57
	Geology	..	..	..	..	3	3	..	..	..	..	..	1	0	..
		101	116	133	120	214	189	229	54	71	107	103	145	83	185
Penny Classes.	Chemistry (Class A)	..	..	..	..	..	..	33	..	..	..	..	..	..	..
	" (Class B)	..	..	..	..	..	..	15	..	..	..	..	..	..	..
	Physical Geography	..	..	..	..	..	..	9	..	..	..	..	..	..	9
	Advanced Arithmetic	13	12	7	7	11	10	12	0	3	1	2	12	10	13
	Elementary "	4	12	19	27	23	24	29	5	12	19	27	21	25	29
	" Singing	..	..	..	23	56	63	81	..	..	..	24	57	62	81
	Penny Lectures	38	31	26	20	39	45	..	39	30	25	20	40	45	..
	Totals	156	171	185	197	343	331	408	98	116	152	176	275	225	317
	Per Centage	27	28	26	23	25	26	26	18	19	21	20	20	17	21

Group	CLASS.	BOYS AT SCHOOL (Probably two-thirds are Sons of Artisans). 1857	1860	1862	1864	1866	1867	1869	SCHOOLMASTERS AND PUPIL TEACHERS. 1857	1860	1862	1864	1866	1867	1869
Science Classes.	Chemistry (Class A)	4	8	5	0	1	3	..	2	2	3	2	2	4	..
	" (Class B)	..	..	..	5	8	4	..	..	..	..	0	5	4	..
	Practical Chemistry	0	0	2	0	0	1	2	0	1	1	0	5	6	7
	Experimental Physics	2	2	2	1	2	1	2	1	1	2	0	1	1	0
	Botany	..	0	0	0	1	0	0	..	1	0	1	2	0	1
	Animal Physiology	..	..	..	..	..	..	0	..	..	..	..	..	..	2
	Practical Plane and Solid Geometry	..	..	..	..	..	..	0	..	..	..	..	..	..	0
	Physical Geography	..	..	..	..	..	0	..	..	..	..	..	..	5	..
	Practical Mechanics	..	..	..	0	0	1	0	..	..	..	0	1	2	1
Mathmcl. Classes.	Algebra	0	2	0	0	0	0	1	0	1	1	1	1	0	0
	Geometry	0	2	0	0	0	0	0	0	0	2	0	2	0	1
Language Classes.	French	8	7	8	0	0	3	4	1	2	1	3	8	4	4
	German	..	..	0	2	0	3	2	..	..	1	0	0	0	1
	Latin	..	..	..	..	5	1	1	..	..	..	..	3	1	1
English Classes.	History	0	5	0	0	0	0	0	0	1	0	0	0	0	0
	Literature	0			0	0	0	0	0			0	0	0	0
	Grammar	..	2	1	0	2	0	0	..	0	0	0	0	1	0
	Writing	..	..	3	2	0	3	1	..	..	0	0	0	0	0
Classes discontinued.	Logic	0	..	..	..	..	..	..	3	..	..	..	..	..	..
	Advanced Singing	..	0	..	..	0	..	0	..	0	..	..	0	..	0
	Geology	..	..	..	..	0	0	..	..	..	..	..	1	0	..
		14	28	21	10	19	20	13	7	9	11	7	31	28	18
Penny Classes.	Chemistry (Class A)	..	..	..	..	..	..	..	..	..	..	..	..	..	..
	" (Class B)	..	..	..	..	..	..	..	..	..	..	..	..	..	..
	Physical Geography	..	..	..	..	..	..	..	..	..	..	..	..	..	..
	Advanced Arithmetic	0	0	4	0	..	..	..	0	0	2	0	..	..	..
	Elementary "	..	..	..	..	..	..	..	..	..	..	..	..	..	..
	" Singing	..	..	..	..	..	..	..	..	..	..	..	..	..	..
	Penny Lectures	..	..	..	..	..	..	..	..	..	..	..	..	..	..
	Totals	14	28	25	10	19	20	13	7	9	13	7	31	28	18
	Per Centage	2	4	3	1	1	1	1	1	1	2	1	2	2	1

Group	CLASS.	TRADESMEN MANUFACTU AND THEIR SONS APPRENTICE (Including Engineers' A 1857	1860	1862	1864	1866
Science Classes.	Chemistry (Class A)	12	9	14	[illegible]	1
	" (Class B)	..	..	..	[illegible]	8
	Practical Chemistry	3	2	3	[illegible]	6
	Experimental Physics	6	5	5	[illegible]	4
	Botany	..	2	1		2
	Animal Physiology	..	..	..	.	..
	Practical Plane and Solid Geometry	..	..	..	.	..
	Physical Geography	..	..	..	.	..
	Practical Mechanics	..	..	..	.	4
Mathmcl. Classes.	Algebra	2	3	4	[illegible]	0
	Geometry	1	3	0	[illegible]	2
Language Classes.	French	7	12	14	[illegible]	10
	German	..	..	4	[illegible]	0
	Latin	..	..	..	.	5
English Classes.	History	1	8	0	5	2
	Literature	4			[illegible]	2
	Grammar	..	4	3	2	2
	Writing	..	..	1	1	0
Classes discontinued.	Logic	1	..	..	.	..
	Advanced Singing	..	0	..	.	1
	Geology	..	..	..	.	4
		37	48	49	4	53
Penny Classes.	Chemistry (Class A)	..	..	..	.	..
	" (Class B)	..	..	..	.	..
	Physical Geography	..	..	..	.	..
	Advanced Arithmetic	1	0	5	2	..
	Elementary "	..	..	..	.	..
	" Singing	..	..	..	.	..
	Penny Lectures	..	..	..	.	..
	Totals	38	48	54	[illegible]	53
	Per Centage	7	8	8	7	[illegible]

* See 1d. Classes.

OCCUPATIONS OF STUDENTS.

FEMALES (…tions not ascertained, …e-half are Daughters of Artisans).					BOYS AT SCHOOL (Probably two-thirds are Sons of Artisans).							SCHOOLMASTERS AND PUPIL TEACHERS.							TRADESMEN AND MANUFACTURERS AND THEIR SONS AND APPRENTICES (Including Engineers' Apprentices).							PROFESSIONAL MEN AND MEDICAL STUDENTS.							TOTALS.							REMARKS
1862	1864	1866	1867	1869	1857	1860	1862	1864	1866	1867	1869	1857	1860	1862	1864	1866	1867	1869	1857	1860	1862	1864	1866	1867	1869	1857	1860	1862	1864	1866	1867	1869	1857	1860	1862	1864	1866	1857	1869	
2	0	0	0	..	4	8	5	0	1	3	..	2	2	3	2	2	4	..	12	9	14	[illegible]	1	10	..	0	0	0	1	2	0	..	50	55	52	23	19	43	..	Established in 1863 } (See 1d. Classes.)
..	3	6	4	..	..	..	..	5	8	4	..	..	..	..	0	5	4	..	..	..	..	1	8	9	..	..	..	..	3	4	1	.	..	..	.	55	82	45	..	
0	0	1	1	1	0	0	2	0	0	1	2	0	1	1	0	5	6	7	3	2	3	.	6	8	5	0	0	0	1	5	1	4	7	5	12	11	24	25	36	
0	1	0	0	1	2	2	2	1	2	1	2	1	1	2	0	1	1	0	6	5	5	[illegible]	4	7	6	0	0	0	0	2	0	0	22	26	17	26	19	24	22	
1	0	2	1	0	..	0	0	0	1	0	0	..	1	0	1	2	0	1	..	2	1		2	0	2	..	0	0	0	0	0	2	..	11	5	8	16	9	14	Established in 1858.
..	..	..	..	0	..	..	..	..	..	..	0	..	..	..	..	..	..	2	..	..	..	.	..	..	1	..	..	..	..	..	..	0	..	..	..	..	..	..	10	" in 1868.
..	..	..	..	0	..	..	..	..	..	..	0	..	..	..	..	..	..	0	..	..	..	.	..	..	2	..	..	..	..	..	..	0	..	..	..	..	..	..	14	" in 1869.
..	..	..	2	..	..	..	..	..	..	0	..	..	..	..	..	..	5	..	..	..	..	.	..	0	..	..	..	..	..	..	0	..	..	..	..	..	..	7	..	" in 1867. (See 1d. Classes.)
..	0	0	0	0	..	..	..	0	0	1	0	..	..	..	0	1	2	1	..	..	..		4	6	3	..	..	..	0	0	0	3	..	..	..	21	20	24	19	" in 1863.
0	0	1	0	0	0	2	0	0	0	0	1	0	1	1	1	1	0	0	2	3	4	.	0	3	3	0	0	0	0	0	0	0	8	18	12	12	21	8	20	
0	0	2	0	0	0	2	0	0	0	0	0	0	0	2	0	2	0	1	1	3	0		2	2	5	0	0	0	0	0	0	0	11	11	8	15	13	3	20	
60	53	60	22	35	8	7	8	0	0	3	4	1	2	1	3	8	4	4	7	12	14	[illegible]	10	3	7	0	0	0	0	0	1	0	169	143	195	157	178	115	134	
17	14	8	9	9	..	..	0	2	0	3	2	..	..	1	0	0	0	1	..	..	4	[illegible]	0	0	5	..	..	1	1	1	2	0	..	..	48	31	28	0	44	Established in 1862.
..	..	11	11	11	..	..	..	..	5	1	1	..	..	..	..	3	1	1	..	..	..	.	5	3	4	..		..	..	0	0	1	..	..	..	..	93	7	48	Established in 1866.
4	4	0	1	4	0	5	0	0	0	0	0	0	1	0	0	0	0	0	1	8	0	[illegible]	2	0	0	0	0	0	0	0	0	0	19	24	21	22	12	2	10	These subjects were taught in one class in the years 1860, 1861, 1862, and 1863.
	3	2	0	[illegible]	0			0	0	0	0	0			0	0	0	0	4			[illegible]	2	0	1	3			2	0	0	0	42			21	19	5	22	
5	15	25	12	2[illegible]	..	2	1	0	2	0	0	..	0	0	0	0	1	0	..	4	3	2	2	2	2	..	0	0	0	0	0	0	..	70	40	51	101	17	93	Established in 1859.
18	10	18	20	32	..	..	3	2	0	3	1	..	..	0	0	0	0	0	..	..	1	1	0	0	0	..	..	0	0	0	0	0	..	..	53	41	52	8	71	Established in 1861.
..	..	..	..	..	0	..	..	..	..	..	..	3	..	..	..	..	..	..	1	..	..	.	..	..	..	0	..	..	..	..	..	..	17	..	..	..	..	.	..	Discontinued in 1858.
..	..	8	..	57	..	0	..	..	0	..	0	..	0	..	..	0	..	0	..	0	..	.	1	..	5	..	0	..	..	0	..	0	..	15	..	..	20	..	150	Established in 1859. Discontinued in 1861. Recommenced in 1866, but discontinued after meeting for one term. Again recommenced in 1869.
..	..	1	0	..	..	..	..	..	0	0	..	..	..	..	..	1	0	..	..	..	..	.	4	1	..	..	..	..	..	1	0	..	..	..	..	..	17	7	..	Established in 1865. Discontinued in 1868.
107	103	145	83	185	14	28	21	10	19	20	13	7	9	11	7	31	28	18	37	48	49	4	53	54	51	3	0	1	8	15	5	10	345	378	463	494	734	95	727	
..	..	..	..	..	..	..	..	..	..	..	..	..	..	..	..	..	..	..	..	..	..	.	..	..	..	..	..	..	..	..	..	..	..	..	..	..	..	.	100	} Quarterly Classes until 1868-9.
..	..	..	..	..	..	..	..	..	..	..	..	..	..	..	..	..	..	..	..	..	..	.	..	..	..	..	..	..	..	..	..	..	..	..	..	..	..	..	45	
..	..	..	..	9	..	..	..	..	..	..	..	..	..	..	..	..	..	..	..	..	..	.	..	..	..	..	..	..	..	..	..	..	..	..	..	..	..	..	48	Quarterly Class until 1867-8.
1	2	12	10	13	0	0	4	0	..	..	..	0	0	2	0	..	..	..	1	0	5	2	..	..	..	0	0	0	0	..	..	..	21	32	29	25	59	50	66	This class was a quarterly one until 1865. It was then established on the 1d. system. It is included in this Table for the purposes of the summary.
19	27	21	25	29	..	..	..	..	..	..	..	..	..	..	..	..	..	..	..	..	..	.	..	..	..	..	..	..	..	..	..	..	21	58	96	132	107	124	145	
..	24	57	62	81	..	..	..	..	..	..	..	..	..	..	..	..	..	..	..	..	..	.	..	..	..	..	..	..	..	..	..	..	..	..	..	116	278	14	407	Established in 1863.
25	20	40	45	..	..	..	..	..	..	..	..	..	..	..	..	..	..	..	..	..	..	.	..	..	..	..	..	..	..	..	..	..	191	154	129	100	193	15	..	Discontinued temporarily to provide room for classes.
152	176	275	225	317	14	28	25	10	19	20	13	7	9	13	7	31	28	18	38	48	54	16	53	54	51	3	0	1	8	15	5	10	578	622	717	867	1371	08	1538	
21	20	20	17	21	2	4	3	1	1	1	1	1	1	2	1	2	2	1	7	8	8	7	4	4	3	0	0	0	1	1	0	0	..	..	..	..	..	..	..	

* See 1d. Classes.

TABLE II.

Shewing the percentage of Students of various occupations attending the Quarterly Classes in the years named.

		Artisans.	Shopmen.	Clerks.	Females.	Boys at School.	Schoolmasters and Pupil Teachers.	Tradesmen and Manufacturers, and their Sons and Apprentices.	Professional Men and Medical Students.
Science Classes ..	1857	23	15	21	3	7	4	27	0
" "	1860	29	14	20	3	10	5	19	0
" "	1862	16	24	7	3	20	6	24	0
" "	1864	35	14	13	3	4	2	26	3
" "	1866	27	17	14	5	6	8	15	8
" "	1867	28	12	18	4	5	11	21	1
" "	1869	30	9	21	2	4	10	16	8
Mathematical Classes	1857	47	0	37	0	0	0	16	0
" "	1860	31	3	28	0	14	3	21	0
" "	1862	25	5	35	0	0	15	20	0
" "	1864	55	0	11	0	0	4	30	0
" "	1866	48	0	28	9	0	9	6	0
" "	1867	56	5	27	0	0	0	12	0
" "	1869	30	5	40	0	2	3	20	0
Language Classes ..	1857	25	12	27	27	5	0	4	0
" "	1860	9	4	42	30	5	1	9	0
" "	1862	10	10	36	32	3	1	8	0
" "	1864	12	6	37	36	1	2	6	0
" "	1866	15	10	38	26	2	4	5	0
" "	1867	14	8	44	22	4	3	3	2
" "	1869	15	4	44	24	3	2	8	0
English Classes ..	1857	32	7	38	10	0	0	8	5
" "	1860	24	10	26	18	8	1	13	0
" "	1862	30	12	28	24	3	0	3	0
" "	1864	35	11	22	24	1	0	6	1
" "	1866	34	6	31	25	1	0	3	0
"	1867	35	6	35	21	2	0	1	0
" "	1869	27	6	34	32	0	0	1	0
Singing Classes ..	1869	32	5	16	45	0	0	2	0

TABLE II.

Shewing the percentage of Students of various occupations attending the Quarterly Classes in the years named.

		Artisans.	Shopmen.	Clerks.	Females.	Boys at School.	Schoolmasters and Pupil Teachers.	Tradesmen and Manufacturers, and their Sons and Apprentices.	Professional Men and Medical Students.
Science Classes ..	1857	23	15	21	3	7	4	27	0
" "	1860	29	14	20	3	10	5	19	0
" "	1862	16	24	7	3	20	6	24	0
" "	1864	35	14	13	3	4	2	26	3
" "	1866	27	17	14	5	6	8	15	8
" "	1867	28	12	18	4	5	11	21	1
" "	1869	30	9	21	2	4	10	16	8
Mathematical Classes	1857	47	0	37	0	0	0	16	0
" "	1860	31	3	28	0	14	3	21	0
" "	1862	25	5	35	0	0	15	20	0
" "	1864	55	0	11	0	0	4	30	0
" "	1866	48	0	28	9	0	9	6	0
" "	1867	56	5	27	0	0	0	12	0
" "	1869	30	5	40	0	2	3	20	0
Language Classes ..	1857	25	12	27	27	5	0	4	0
" "	1860	9	4	42	30	5	1	9	0
" "	1862	10	10	36	32	3	1	8	0
" "	1864	12	6	37	36	1	2	6	0
" "	1866	15	10	38	26	2	4	5	0
" "	1867	14	8	44	22	4	3	3	2
" "	1869	15	4	44	24	3	2	8	0
English Classes ..	1857	32	7	38	10	0	0	8	5
" "	1860	24	10	26	18	8	1	13	0
" "	1862	30	12	28	24	3	0	3	0
" "	1864	35	11	22	24	1	0	6	1
" "	1866	34	6	31	25	1	0	3	0
"	1867	35	6	35	21	2	0	1	0
" "	1869	27	6	34	32	0	0	1	0
Singing Classes ..	1869	32	5	16	45	0	0	2	0

www.ingramcontent.com/pod-product-compliance
Lightning Source LLC
Chambersburg PA
CBHW082059070426
42452CB00052B/2754
* 9 7 8 1 5 3 5 8 0 3 8 6 1 *